Advance

Acrostic Poetry: The

Beginning with ancient acrosti... remarkable book shares the fasc... Michael Croland's well chronicl... woven through society's history. This rewarding collection of poems is a welcome gift for spreading interest and delight in acrostics.

—Avis Harley, author of *African Acrostics: A Word in Edgeways*

"There's a first time for everything," they say, and that is apparently true for Michael Croland's gathering of poems written in the venerable verse form called "acrostics." . . . Croland has treated the subject exhaustively in this interesting volume.

—Lewis Turco, author of *The Book of Forms*

Far from basic poetry, acrostics, the introduction notes, "have an ancient history in Latin, Greek, and Hebrew" and transcend the constrained form. From Blackwell's three-line acrostic about the sun to Chilton's lengthy poem about The Lord's Prayer, readers will savor poems on assorted subjects from both famous authors and unknown writers.

—Lisa M. Bolt Simons, author of *Acrostic Poems*

Aficionados of wordplay will delight in this long overdue compendium of an often undervalued art form, which also discusses its history and highlights, along with variations ancient and modern such as the hidden acrostics in Shakespeare, Joyce, and, not unexpectedly, Lewis Carroll.

—Mark Burstein, president emeritus of
The Lewis Carroll Society of North America

It's a poetic party on paper for Word Nerds like me, and a must-read for devotees of the form.

—Brian P. Cleary, author of *Bow-Tie Pasta: Acrostic Poems*

ACROSTIC POETRY
The First-Ever Anthology

DOVER THRIFT EDITIONS

Edited by
Michael Croland

DOVER PUBLICATIONS
GARDEN CITY, NEW YORK

DOVER THRIFT EDITIONS

GENERAL EDITOR: SUSAN L. RATTINER
EDITOR OF THIS VOLUME: MICHAEL CROLAND

To Tamara and Robin

Bibliographical Note

Acrostic Poetry: The First-Ever Anthology is a new work, first published by Dover Publications in 2023.

Library of Congress Cataloging-in-Publication Data

Names: Croland, Michael, editor.
Title: Acrostic poetry : the first-ever anthology / edited by Michael Croland.
Description: Garden City, New York : Dover Publications, 2023. | Series: Dover thrift editions | Includes bibliographical references. | Summary: "In this first-ever anthology, more than eighty acrostics show the versatility of a storied poetic form that dates back to ancient times. In standard acrostics, the initial letters of successive lines spell out words when read vertically"—Provided by publisher.
Identifiers: LCCN 2022056715 | ISBN 9780486850429 (trade paperback) | ISBN 0486850420 (trade paperback)
Subjects: LCSH: Acrostics. | LCGFT: Acrostics (Poetry)
Classification: LCC PN6371 .A37 2023 | DDC 808.81—dc23/eng/20230302
LC record available at https://lccn.loc.gov/2022056715

Manufactured in the United States of America
85042001   2023
www.doverpublications.com

Contents

ACKNOWLEDGMENTS

Thank you to Peter Lenz and Susan Rattiner for your support of this anthology. Thank you to the rest of the Dover team, especially Peter Donahue, Janet Kopito, and Marie Zaczkiewicz.

Thank you to the Massachusetts Historical Society for providing "What wou'd my feeble Muse so boldly fly?" and "Recipe for the Spleen, From an Old Woman," both by Louisa Catherine Adams, from the Adams Family Papers. Thank you, Amanda Norton and Hannah Elder, for your guidance and assistance.

Thank you to Vefa Bozos, Kelly Cobble of Adams National Historical Park, David Perle, and Jonah Schrogin for your help.

Thank you, Tamara, for your love and patience.

Poetically speaking, here's a shout-out to Robin, Mom, Jack, Nancy, Benjamin, Alan, Marla, Dan, Lisa, Zachary, and Zoey.

INTRODUCTION
AT THE TIP OF THE VERSE

In a standard acrostic poem, the initial letters of successive lines spell out a word or group of words when read vertically. Variations include having the last letter of each line or a diagonal sequence of letters spell out words. The acrostic has attracted top-tier writers, poets laureate, and even presidents. It is well past time for this storied poetic form to get the spotlight.

The English word "acrostic" is based on the Latin *acrostichis*, which derives from the Greek *akron* (end) and *stikhos* (line of verse). A common translation from the Greek is "at the tip of the verse."

Acrostics have an ancient history in Latin, Greek, and Hebrew. They might have originated as a mnemonic device for oral transmission of texts, with alphabet poems as the oldest version. Numerous examples appear in the Bible. Writers of acrostics in Latin include Plautus, who had acrostics at the beginning of his plays and died in 184 BCE; Commodianus, who composed eighty acrostics in the fourth century CE; and St. Augustine, who penned an alphabetical hymn in 393 CE.

Some key highlights of the development of acrostics in English are from a handful of books. In 1599, Sir John Davies paved the way for the tradition of using the form to praise someone's name by writing twenty-six acrostics spelling out Queen Elizabeth I's name in *Hymnes of Astræa in Acrosticke Verse*. In 1637, Mary Fage followed suit with 420 acrostics about royals and noblemen in *Fames Roule*. Between 1855 and 1876, Robert Blackwell, W. P. Chilton, Charles Vaughan Grinfield, and D. F. Lockerby published notable acrostic books, accounting for numerous selections in this anthology. Also in the nineteenth century, Edgar Allan Poe and Lewis Carroll wrote multiple innovative acrostics, and both beloved authors have their own chapters in this volume.

Most acrostics spell out someone's name. "I frame/Exact in capitals your golden name," boasted the English Romantic poet John Keats in an acrostic to his sister. Subjects include famous figures, such as monarchs and presidents, as well as people close to the poets. Some of the most common poetic themes, including love, religion, and nature, are also standard fare.

In this day and age, acrostic poems are often thought of as creative writing exercises for children as well as adults who don't have much experience writing poetry. The built-in structure helps guide novices to construct poems. In *Hunting the Snark: A Compendium of New Poetic Terminology*, Robert Peters declared, "This venerable form, usually relegated to warm-up exercises in beginning poetry workshops, is not much used by serious poets." Many people dismiss the form as rudimentary poetry because of this association, unaware of its long-standing history and vast potential.

Hallmarks of the Form

A great acrostic is a great poem that happens to be an acrostic. Many of the best acrostics rely on conventions commonly found in other types of verse, including rhyme and meter. When a poem succeeds in spite of the limitations of the form, especially in conjunction with skillfully crafted rhyme and meter, it is impressive and commendable because of the extra constraint.

Coordinating with the initial letter of each line—or letters elsewhere—is a creative challenge. Acrostic poets work within these confines. As with rhyme, meter, and alliteration, some poets hit the ball out of the park with the acrostic challenge and others strike out. Schoolchildren's widespread failure to create masterpieces should not be an indictment of the form when accomplished poets have succeeded so brilliantly.

An acrostic sometimes spells out the same word that appears in the poem's title or initial line. That word typically reinforces the message of the poem. This is consistent with the crucial role of repetition in poetry. In *A Poet's Craft*, Annie Finch posited, "The powerful and pleasurable technique of repetition is central to the very nature of poetry." She explained, "Repetition, in all its infinite and complex shapes, makes language more than the sum of its parts. And the repetitions of poetry—meter, rhyme, refrain, the free-verse line break—also communicate with the rhythms of our hearts and breath and the repeating motions of our work, love, and play." The repetition inherent in acrostics helps convey meaning and emphasize key points. A message resonates more if it is expressed multiple times.

Standard acrostics, in which a word is spelled out by the initial letters, can be remembered and recited more easily than most poems. This is especially true of alphabet poems, which helps explain their prominence in ancient writing. Acrostics are so intertwined with memory recall that one of the most common types of mnemonic devices is acrostic mnemonics. While examples are typically not in verse, they have an acrostic structure. Many children learned the order of the planets in our solar system—when Pluto was still considered a planet—with this acrostic sentence: "My very energetic mother just served us nine pizzas." The mnemonic potential of acrostics enabled two poets who have multiple selections in this anthology to compose poems in their heads and dictate them to amanuenses. Before he learned to write, George Moses Horton, a slave, thought up acrostics while doing farmwork and later dictated the content to university students. Grinfield was visually impaired, if not totally blind, and dictated the poems to a woman named Gertrude, presumably his wife.

Almost all acrostics that spell out people's names present their subjects positively. Only four selections in this volume portray their subjects in a negative light, and these poems stand out because they are against the grain. The members of this exclusive club are Benedict Arnold, an officer who betrayed the Continental Army in the Revolutionary War; Napoleon, an emperor with a thirst for conquest; John Randolph, a congressional firebrand with a few screws loose; and Martin Van Buren, a president who was widely panned because of a financial crisis.

A poem can be both an acrostic and another form. Naysayers about acrostics might have to reconsider their poetic biases for selections that are also sonnets, distinguished verse with fourteen rhyming lines. Several acrostic sonnets appear in this volume, including poems by Poe, Wilfrid Scawen Blunt, James Gates Percival, and Nathaniel Parker Willis. Other amalgamated forms—including haiku, limericks, and villanelles with acrostic features—can be found on the internet.

Many poets only spell out words that they can pull off seamlessly. Some acrostics have letters that are difficult to work with, and the resulting lines can come across as forced. The worst culprit is X. Some poets make obscure references (e.g., Xerxes), and others delete the e in the prefix "ex-," either with or without an apostrophe (e.g., "Xcellent," "'Xcelling").

Many acrostics have straightforward titles, but few have creative ones. If a poem appeared in the source material with a generic title such as "An Acrostic," the title has been omitted.

Scope

In compiling the first anthology of acrostic poetry, the editor found it necessary to limit the scope. The goal was to present an organized, readable collection of acrostics, showing the history and highlights of the form, for a general audience. If the line were not drawn somewhere, this volume would have been unwieldy.

All the poems in this book were originally written in English. The acrostics are all poems for the sake of being poems; acrostic puzzles that are primarily intended as puzzles are not included. Acrostic prose is excluded, as are acrostic poems where the initial letters of couplets or stanzas, rather than each line, spell out words. Acrostics spelling out the names of unfamous subjects are excluded unless the poet is well-known. All selections are in the public domain and were originally written by 1927.

An Inconvenient Truth

Two poets in this volume supported the Confederate States of America (CSA). The CSA seceded from the US, fought against the US in the Civil War, and championed the slavery of human beings.

Blackwell featured acrostics about every US president and state plus a host of other subjects in a book published in 1868. The following year, he published a work with a lot of the same content. That version contained acrostics praising Confederate subjects, including Robert E. Lee, Jefferson Davis, and Richmond. Blackwell's poems are essential reading for anyone interested in acrostics, and selections can be found in several chapters. This anthology does not include any of his pro-CSA material.

Chilton was a representative from Alabama in the Confederate Congress. His book-length acrostics spelling out the Lord's Prayer and every state in the US were published posthumously. The former, the most ambitious acrostic ever written, appears in this volume in its entirety.

Excluding Blackwell and Chilton would not be prudent. Their contributions to acrostic poetry are too significant.

ALPHABET POEMS

An alphabet poem, or abecedarian, is an acrostic where the first letter of each line, couplet, or stanza sequentially spells out the alphabet.

Historically, alphabet poems flourished in other languages. In Hebrew, there are fourteen alphabet poems in the Old Testament—including four out of five chapters in the Book of Lamentations—and three in the Dead Sea Scrolls. Each stanza in Psalm 119, penned by King David, begins with a new letter, and all eight lines within the stanza start with that letter. In a survey of alphabet poems, Nyr Indictor noted that they are "relatively easily committed to memory." According to Indictor, Psalm 119, which addresses Jewish law, "renders a complex body of knowledge more accessible" to a populace that is not entirely literate. In *Dictionary of the Old Testament,* C. J. Fantuzzo explained, "An acrostic is complete, 'from A to Z'; yet an acrostic limits, providing closure, assuring the reader that enough has been said." In addition, there were nearly a score of abecedarians in Latin hymns—including an alphabetical psalm written by St. Augustine—and at least three in Greek hymns.

Alphabet poems by two renowned writers are excluded from this chapter because they were not originally written entirely in English. The earliest known specimen in English is "An ABC" by Geoffrey Chaucer. Apparently composed in 1369, it is a translation of a poem written in French circa 1330. Jonathan Swift wrote an English poem spelling out the Greek alphabet in the 1720s, likely as part of a bet.

Whereas most alphabet poems in the last two centuries were written for children—and many are not impressive as poetry when they are removed from their pedagogical and illustrated contexts—the following selections offer a droll, clever spin on an ancient poetic form. "Title-Page for a Book of Extracts from Many Authors" offers alluring alliteration, even if it might come across as forced. Edward Lear, who is best remembered for his limericks, wrote a dozen alphabet poems. "A Christmas Alphabet" by Carolyn Wells, a champion of whimsical writing, has found a second life as the text of several Christmas picture books published in recent decades.

1

Title-Page for a Book of Extracts from Many Authors

ANONYMOUS

Astonishing Anthology from Attractive Authors.
Broken Bits from Bulky Brains.
Choice Chunks from Chaucer to Channing.
Dainty Devices from Diverse Directions.
Echoes of Eloquence from Eminent Essayists.
Fragrant Flowers from Fields of Fancy.
Gems of Genius Gloriously Garnished.
Handy Helps from Head and Heart.
Illustrious Intellects Intelligently Interpreted.
Jewels of Judgment and Jets of Jocularity.
Kindlings to Keep from the King to the Kitchen.
Loosened Leaves from Literary Laurels.
Magnificent Morsels from Mighty Minds.
Numerous Nuggets from Notable Noodles.
Oracular Opinions Officiously Offered.
Prodigious Points from Powerful Pens.
Quirks and Quibbles from Queer Quarters.
Rare Remarks Ridiculously Repeated.
Suggestive Squibs from Sundry Sources.
Tremendous Thoughts on Thundering Topics.
Utterances from Uppermost for Use and Unction.
Valuable Views in Various Voices.
Wisps of Wit in a Wilderness of Words.
Xcellent Xtracts Xactly Xpressed.
Yawnings and Yearnings for Youthful Yankees.
Zeal and Zest from Zoroaster to Zimmerman.

A tumbled down, and hurt his Arm, against a bit of wood.

B said, "My Boy, O! do not cry; it cannot do you good!"

C said, "A Cup of Coffee hot can't do you any harm."

D said, "A Doctor should be fetched, and he would cure the arm."

E said, "An Egg beat up with milk would quickly make him well."

F said, "A Fish, if broiled, might cure, if only by the smell."

G said, "Green Gooseberry fool, the best of cures I hold."

H said, "His Hat should be kept on, to keep him from the cold."

I said, "Some Ice upon his head will make him better soon."

J said, "Some Jam, if spread on bread, or given in a spoon!"

K said, "A Kangaroo is here,—this picture let him see."

L said, "A Lamp pray keep alight, to make some barley tea."

M said, "A Mulberry or two might give him satisfaction."

N said, "Some Nuts, if rolled about, might be a slight attraction."

O said, "An Owl might make him laugh, if only it would wink."

P said, "Some Poetry might be read aloud, to make him think."

Q said, "A Quince I recommend,—a Quince, or else a Quail."

R said, "Some Rats might make him move, if fastened by their tail."

S said, "A Song should now be sung, in hopes to make him laugh!"

T said, "A Turnip might avail, if sliced or cut in half!"

U said, "An Urn, with water hot, place underneath his chin!"

V said, "I'll stand upon a chair, and play a Violin!"

W said, "Some Whisky-Whizzgigs fetch, some marbles and a ball!"

X said, "Some double XX ale would be the best of all!"

Y said, "Some Yeast mixed up with salt would make a perfect plaster!"

Z said, "Here is a box of Zinc! Get in, my little master!

"We'll shut you up! We'll nail you down! We will, my little master!

"We think we've all heard quite enough of this your sad disaster!"

A Christmas Alphabet

CAROLYN WELLS

A is for Apple that hangs on the tree.
B is for Bells that chime out in glee.
C is for Candy to please boys and girls.
D is for Dolls with long flaxen curls.
E is for Evergreens decking the room.
F is for Flowers of exquisite perfume.
G is for Gifts that bring us delight.
H is for Holly with red berries bright.
I is for Ice so shining and clear.
J is the Jingle of bells far and near.
K is Kriss Kringle with fur cap and coat.
L is for Letters the children all wrote.
M is for Mistletoe, shining like wax.
N is for Nuts which Grandpapa cracks.
O is for Oranges, yellow and sweet.
P for Plum Pudding, a holiday treat.
Q, the Quadrille in which each one must dance.
R for the Reindeer that gallop and prance.
S is for Snow that falls silently down.
T is for Turkey, so tender and brown.
U is for Uproar that goes on all day.
V is for Voices that carol a lay.
W, for Wreaths hung up on the wall.
X is for Xmas, with pleasures for all.
Y is for Yule-log that burns clear and bright.
Z is for Zest shown from morning till night.

KINGS AND QUEENS

The tradition of basing an acrostic on a person's name originated with extolling a monarch, and other British poets followed suit. Two seminal early acrostic books had a royal focus.

In addition to being a lawyer and government official in England and Ireland, Sir John Davies was an Elizabethan poet who promoted order and authority in his verse. His *Hymnes of Astræa in Acrosticke Verse* (1599) is a series of twenty-six acrostics spelling out "Elisabetha Regina," the Latin translation of "Queen Elizabeth." "Astræa" also refers to her name. In *The Oxford Guide to Word Games*, Tony Augarde noted that Davies "established the practice of praising somebody by writing an acrostic using their name," which accounts for the majority of the acrostics in this volume and the predominant association with the form. In *The Pursuit of Poetry*, Louis Untermeyer hailed Davies's "genuine tribute" as "ingenious."

In *Fames Roule* (1637), Mary Fage shares 420 acrostics about not just the reigning king and queen but also "Dukes, Marquesses, Earles, Viscounts, Bishops, Barons, Privie Counsellors, Knights of the Garter, and Judges." For princes, for example, Fage explained that she "present[s] each of you with a glimpse of his owne glory naturally innated in your Names," calling herself the "honourer of your vertues." Critics have been harsh. In *Women's Writing in English*, Patricia Demers described Fage's verse as "tortured" and "laboured and taxing." In her acrostic about King Charles I, *V* can function as either *V* or *U*.

The final three selections were published when the monarchs depicted were on the throne, in 1793, 1793, and 1846, respectively.

Hymne XIII: Of Her Mind

Sir John Davies

Earth now adiew, my ravisht thought
Lifted to heav'n, sets thee at nought;
Infinit is my longing,
Secrets of Angels to be taught,
And things to heav'n belonging.

Brought downe from heav'n of Angels kind,
Even now do I admire her mind:
This is my contemplation,
Her cleare sweet *Spirit* which is refind,
Above Humane *Creation*.

Rich Sun-beame of th'æternall light,
Excellent *Soule,* how shall I wright;
Good Angels make me able;
I cannot see but by your eye,
Nor, but by your tongue, Signifie,
A thing so Admirable.

Hymne XXIII: Of Her Justice

SIR JOHN DAVIES

Exil'd *Astræa* is come againe,
Lo here she doth all things maintaine
In *number, waight*, and *measure*:
She rules us with delightfull paine,
And we obey with pleasure.

By *Love* shee rules more then by *Law*,
Even her great *mercy* breedeth awe:
This is her Sword and Scepter,
Herewith she hearts did ever draw,
And this Guard ever kept her.

Reward doth sit in her right hand:
Each Vertue thence takes her Garland
Gather'd in Honors garden:
In her left hand (wherein should be
Nought but the Sword) sits Clemencie,
And conquers Vice with pardon.

To the Kings Most Excellent Majestie: Carolvs Stvarte

MARY FAGE

Charles our great Monarch, on my bended knee,
AV! much-admiring at your Majesty!
Render I to your sacred Personage
Of your most Princely vertues, this true gage:
Lustrous your beames of brightnes, like true *Sol*,
Vailes the beholders eyes, or dazels all,
Shining in glory over all the Earth;

Shewing your light onto the greatest birth:
The severall planets of our firmament,
Vertues nobility, their lustre lent,
AV! have from you, our true and lively Sunne,
Releeving with your heat, where ere you come.
Thus just true fervour in your person pace,
Enliv'ning all things in your *SOL'S TRV TRACE*.

JOHN ANKETELL

Kind Providence, attentive to our good,
In tender mercy deals us cloaths and food;
Nor less beneficent in other things,
Gives us for governor the best of kings.
Guided by motives of the purest kind,
Endu'd with ev'ry excellence of mind;
On virtue's base intent to found his name,
Religion unaffected stamps his fame:
Grac'd with each principle to prove him great,
England's lov'd monarch holds the reins of state.
Touch'd by the orphan's, or the widow's grief,
His lib'ral hand administers relief.
Ever observant of his children's weal,
The parent glows with amiable zeal:
His bliss compleated by a matchless spouse,
In spotless truth he pays his marriage vows.
Respected, equitable, mild, and just,
Deathless his worth shall soar above the dust.

Could my fond thoughts a proper utt'rance find,
How would they praise the first of womankind!
Adorn'd with ev'ry excellence and grace,
Roy'lty holds in her but a second place.
Like a good angel hast'ning from the skies.
On blessings' wings *Charlotte* to *England* flies,
The virtues which her heav'nly form complete,
To rank give worth, and dignity to state.
Endu'd with female gentleness of breast,
Quiescent the tumultuous passions rest.
Unfeign'd devotion, void of showy art,
Elates her soul, and animates her heart.
Exalted feelings, and maternal love,
Nourish'd by piety, her merits prove.
Oppress'd by indigence, or sunk in grief,
From her each wretch is sure to find relief.
Guided by sense each weakness to controul,
Reason invigorates and fills her soul.
Enrich'd by wisdom, and chaste honor's laws,
Admiring millions join in just applause.
The jarring int'rests which at courts are seen,
Besiege in vain *Great Britain's* darling queen.
Rais'd up by God our manners to amend,
In grateful strains our thanks should heav'nward tend:
Taught by her bright example, age and youth,
Attach'd sincerely to the paths of truth;
In graceful humbleness their lives shall lead,
Nor fear the shafts which lay them with the dead.

Rosina Amelia Noah

Virtuous maiden, gentle, mild, serene,
In wisdom, judgment, noblest actions seen,
Council and ruler, England's hope and pride,
To sway the sceptre, and a Nation guide;
Oh, may thy heart with charity encrease,
Rich in those virtues, justice, mercy, peace
Irradiate glories, crown thy royal head,
And heaven refulgent, all its blessings shed.

Omniscient power, might, infinite, divine,
Unerring wisdom, attributes sublime;
Religion guide, while earthly honors shine.

Beatified and glorious seraphs guard thy throne,
Love in each breast, no treachery, hatred known,
Each subject faithful, every heart thine own,
So may thy reign be long and happy to the end,
Salvation thine, celestial gifts descend;
Eternal high, thy soul to heaven may rise.
Diadem may gain, where virtue never dies.

Quick to obey thy royal sovereign word,
Union and peace, thro' all the land is heard,
England, rejoice! for time's rude hand defies,
Ever true virtue lives, when youth and beauty dies,
Now Briton's triumph, Victory's banner flies.

PRESIDENTS

Just as British poets praised monarchs with acrostics, their American counterparts have given presidents the same treatment. While acrostics about presidents appear in numerous sources, this chapter focuses on excerpts from two books that featured acrostics about every American president to date. Subjects include some of the most revered presidents as well as others where the poets succeeded in showing a side that deserves to be seen.

Robert Blackwell's *Original Acrostics, on All the States and Presidents of the United States, and Various Other Subjects, Religious, Political and Personal* (1868) spells out the name of each president. While the book comprehensively addresses all the states and presidents, it is more remarkable for the breadth of other topics, which are included in three other chapters in this volume. Blackwell's scathing portrayal of Martin Van Buren relates to the eighth president's role in a financial crisis.

D. F. Lockerby's *Acrostical Pen Portraits of the Eighteen Presidents of the United States* (1876) coincided with the nation's centennial. Each selection begins with the president's name and birthplace, and some contain much more information. The verse achieves a sustained narrative that is rare for acrostics. Lockerby explained that he had more to say about some presidents, including George Washington, because "there are more events of great moment crowded into the life of some than of others." The text contains pejorative references to Native Americans and other groups that may be deemed offensive by today's standards. They should be viewed in the historical context of the wars that are discussed.

Thomas Jefferson

ROBERT BLACKWELL

Threatened by foes on land and sea,
Heeding not the powers that be,
Our fathers, struggling to be free,
Made us renowned, by giving thee
A pen to write a declaration,
Scorning chains and degradation,
Just in time to save a nation,
Expressing worth by demonstration;
Flinching not, with pen in hand,
For us so boldly took thy stand,
Elevated by command,
Rolled the ink to save our land.
So long as stars and stripes shall wave
O'er this land of the *fair and brave*,
Nations will respect thy grave.

Martin Van Buren

ROBERT BLACKWELL

More fool than wise, more knave than saint,
And yet he had so many charms,
Reclining on his chair of ease,
The people took him to their arms;
In all his glory they saw him rise,
Not clothed with virtue, but with disguise.

Vows he broke from day to day,
And though he made a great display,
No good of him can mortal say.

But still from us he homage claims,
Unmindful of his traitorous aims;
Robed in the garments of a foe,
Enticing men with him to go—
Not to heaven, but down below.

Great, consecrated and immortal name,
Emblem of glory, honor, truth and fame,
O'er all his fellows—see! he grandly towers,
Rising amid the great—excels their powers.
Great his designs in time of war or peace,
Enlisted wholly, solely, for the Land's increase.

Within his own great and prophetic heart,
A nation is equipped in every part.
See! when the hour to strike for Freedom comes,
He draws his sword; and first among the sons,
Immortal sons of glory, takes his place.
Nations admire, kings rush to his embrace.
Greatest of all the nations forth is brought,
The new-born nation Washington had sought.
O'er the broad continent he casts his eye,
Now free forever—he is free to die.

Born of old English stock of noble fame,
Ranks high his family and ancestral name.
In early years his father dies, and he
Depends on mother, what his life shall be.
Greatest of blessings is a mother good,
Early to feed the soul with wholesome food:
She as a mother without equal stood.

Careful, she taught him every wise behest;
Religious precepts—the purest and the best.
Early to school she sent her son, 'tis true—
Each school day course, her course did far out-do.
Kind-hearted youth—yet wore a front of iron

Puts not away the lovely, witching siren,
Of rules for conduct had a hundred fold
To guide, to fashion, every thought to mould.
Of books, the Bible and Sir Matthew Hale
Made his first study; these o'er all prevail.
An expert was in mathematics, too,
Classical colleges he never knew.

When sixteen years of age, his school days end,
Early in life to business must attend.
So trained in virtue, famed for love of truth,
'Tis his to form the model son and youth.
Modest and mighty, he grew up a man
Of noblest purpose, both to act and plan,
Rich in the noblest feelings of a manly heart,
Ever he acts a great and noble part.
Like Joseph, David, Daniel, who of old
Are seen to shine like stars of purest gold.
Nor can we rank less worthy him to-day,
Deep in whose heart the same high motives sway.

Careful that saintly mother taught her son:
Of all her work this wast most carefully done.
Unconsciously she trained a leader great,
Nor dreams she that a President he'll make;
To her great joy, she lives to see the day
Young George, her son, this honor bore away.

Virginia's hills and vales surveyed, and solved
Intricate problems which estates involved.
Remiss to duty—he was never charged,
Genial to all, his heart and mind enlarged.
In unity, he with his brother dwelt,
No discord marred the joy these brothers felt.
Induced was he to seek a naval fame,
As oft his brother had advised the same.

Fortune decided otherwise, for he
A mother's counsel heeded, as we see
The British navy lost a good recruit,
Half of a continent this from Britain took.
E'en now the seed is cast within the field,
Rising in glory will a nation yield.

O'er mountain heights, through valleys, and o'er plains,
Fairfax, his friend, with George delights to range.

Hark! in the West the din of war we hear,
Indians with French 'gainst Britain's power appear.
Selected by Dinwiddie to convey

Cross mountain wilds, o'er pathless miles away,
One single message to the French commander,
Unaw'd he undertakes this toil of grandeur,
Nor goes in vain—selects the best location
To rear his future forts, by observation.
Raised for the frontier are three hundred men,
Young George, Lieutenant Colonel, over them.

The brave young colonel, with but part his troops,
Has gone to see how frontier service looks.
Ere his arrival hostile French again

Great Britain's power would scornfully disdain.
Ready for action under Jummonville,
Enlisted for a fight, he sets his will.
A skirmish, that is all, he routs the foe,
To flight they're put; their leader lying low.

Midst these fatigues, the first commander dies
In Washington, command-in-chief relies.
Lacking no part that makes a chieftain true.
Increased his army with fresh troops we view,
'Tis his to march his force to Fort Duquesne,
And there attack the strong French garrison.
Retreat from this, he finds his only course,
Yields he to numbers, in far superior force.

Comes back and halts at Fort Necessity,
His gallantry displays and bravery.
Attacked by French and Indian forces strong,
Matches his far inferior numbers long,
Plants himself in the front line of the fight,
In action fearless leads, with dauntless might.
O'ercome by numbers superior to his own,
Now yields the fort; in bravery yields to none.

Old England now her bravest general sends,
French troops to banish from her soil intends.

A grand display—Virginia's rangers come,
Marshalled with regulars; Braddock and Washington
Eagerly take the field for Fort Duquesne.
Ranked next to Braddock, Washington is seen.
Indifferent to the crafty Indian's guile,
Careless is Braddock, thinking of no wile,
An Indian ambuscade he feareth not,
Nor will he learn, by Washington though taught.

Indians behind the trees now lie in wait,
Nor will he know till they have sealed his fate.
Dashing forward, his men he leads in pride,
Entering the forest—now from every side
Pouring volley on volley, Braddock he falls dead.
Each tree an Indian hides; the woods run red.
Nothing is left for them that now survive,
Defeated thus by such a dire surprise,
Except retreat—the best that they can do;
No other course for them is left in view.
Crafty the Indian tried, and tried in vain,
Each deadly shot for Washington took aim.

At his brave heart leveled each musket shot,
Now, e'en his coat these bullets entered not.
Determined now, the French troops they must rout

Forbes, Brigadier General, is sent out;
Instructed, goes to capture Fort Duquesne.
Return they did not, Forbes and Washington,
Sweeping before them every barrier down,
Till no French fort in all the West is found.

Place Washington, of heroes, first among;
Reared thus a warrior, when the pressure comes,
Exacting taxes from Columbia's sons—
Sad error, which by Parliament was made,
Induced the colonies a war to wage.
Deep in the heart of Washington there grew
Eternal principles of justice true.
Now Patrick Henry by his heart appeals
This heart can pierce, which quivering feels,

One, quick the other, flies each fiery shaft
Fast through the heart, where leaden shot ne'er pass'd.

"To arms!" the cry resounds all o'er the land,
Hear soon the clash of arms on every hand.
E'en now at Boston and at Lexington,

Unwilling warfare has ere this begun.
Now all convened in solemn conclave met,
In awful firm resolve each man is set.
The conscript fathers, there did dare to rise,
E'en though darkness deep should lower the skies,
Determined they, for Independence swore,

Signed, sealed, proclaimed their purpose evermore.
To Washington, the Congress wisely gave
A place, the highest, and the country save.
To bring his country quick and sure relief,
Exalted is to the command-in-chief,
Saves the whole nation, and defeats her foes.

Firmly upon his purpose bent he goes
In rapid marches to Boston, makes his way
Ready, all things prepares, as best he may.
Severely taxed, amid such vast confusion,
'Tis his to rid the place of Howe's intrusion.

Incessant toil, all through the hours of night,
Now Dorchester, he fortifies her heights;

When suddenly the British troops embark
All trace of whom is gone before 'tis dark.
Redoubled force the British bring to bear

Around New York; they're bound to triumph there.
Now poorly clad, his army bare and small,
Dares Washington, with new recruits and all,

Forward to march, this stronghold to defend,
In face of all that Britain Great may send.
Regardless of her war ships, soldiers brave
See Washington intent New York to save.
They land their troops, the ships command the shore.

Impending ruin for raw recruits in store,
Not able to contend, he bears defeat.

Places his men, wise course, in full retreat;
Embarks his troops 'neath cover of the night
Arrives in New York safe, the foe in sight.
Cross o'er he must, and in New Jersey come,
Each moment counts, as flying soldiers run.

A series of disasters and defeat
Now mark his course—his only hope retreat;
Depressed and starving soldiers now desert,

Fears and distress bear down on every heart.
In no respect is Washington dismayed,
Resolute, sends to Congress for fresh aid;
Secures, for soldiers, rations and fair pay,
Tasks his brave heart by night as well by day.

In winter storms, harassed upon the rear,
Nights cold and stormy and no shelter near.

To Trenton comes, but dare not spend the night,
He must continue still his pressing flight.
Embarks his troops at night. The Delaware

High, rapid, full of ice floes now must bear
Each almost naked soldier on her breast;
A bloody foe is in the rear—no rest
Remains this side, the dark and turgid stream,
'Tis life or death for them to choose between.
Stay here and die—go o'er the stream and live.

Of choice, the latter they prefer; and give,
Fearless of danger in the darkling night,

Themselves to grapple with the water's might.
Heaven smiles o'er them; and God's angels keep
Each soldier safe—borne o'er the swelling deep—

Pure angel bands these vigils ever keep.
Enforcements now from Philadelphia come
Of noblest men—the father and the son.
Pleasing to see, New Jersey sends her share,
Lifting from Washington a load of care.
Ere morn will dawn, the tide of war will turn,

And Lord Cornwallis will in anger burn.
Let George alone—no greater general born;
With dextrous move Cornwallis will be shorn,
And haughty British troops will yet retreat,
Yielding before our troops will bear defeat.
Soon they will break and run on "flying feet."

D. F. LOCKERBY

Zealous soldier, true patriot, modest and pure,
Achieving a fame that shall ever endure;
Claim we the highest renown for thee,
History fails to present one more worthy than thee.
As lieutenant he enters the army to serve,
Routs the western Indians with courage and nerve;
Yields neither to savages, hunger nor fire,

To accomplish his purpose, his only desire.
A command of the army, the southwest division,
You see to this brave fighting hero is given;
Leaving Florida, now to Fort Jessup he goes,
O'erlooking the Mexican, fierce Texan foes.
Rearing his quarters at Corpus Christi,

Observation at first, occupation by and by.
Remained several months, next to Rio Grande goes,
Arrives after seventeen days' marching close;
Now Matamoras opposite raises his flag,
Grand music is pealing, Yankee Doodle's no drag.
Encamped in the sight and range of the foe,

Calmly he waits for Ampudia to show
Of which he'll make choice, Peace or War in his mind,
Until a true boundary both the governments find.
Not willing to wait, the Mexicans pour
To this side of the stream, to our side of the shore;
You now see their General Arista in haste

Viewing our troops, whom he thinks to lay waste.
In the meantime, when ready, our general says "Fire!"
Red gory the field, beaten foes soon retire.
Grim with the smoke of Pal' Alto's burnt plain,
In confusion, 'mid fire, they rally again;
Now pressed by our troops—not a moment's delay—
In glory our arms win the fight of the day,
A victory brilliant by Taylor is won,

He follows the foe, in disorder who've run.
Early next morning, the foe for defense,
Resaco la Palma is the place they intrench.
Out of this natural fortress they're driven,

On every side pressed, their army is riven.
Forced to surrender, Matamoras yields,

'Tis his to press forward to new gory fields.
He next attacks Monterey looming up in the west.
Environed by batt'ries, yet he dares to invest.

More brilliant a victory soldier ne'er won,
Encountering such odds—Balaklava's outdone.
'Xcelling e'en this, Buena Vista is fought,
In which, with a few raw recruits lately got,
Compassed now round about twenty thousand and more,
A note to "surrender," Santa Anna sends o'er.
"Not so," replies Taylor; the battle fires flash,

With confidence bold, on the Mexicans dash.
And by masterly strategy, skill, and fine tact,
Ruin'd and beaten, the foes driven back.

"A little more grape, Captain Bagg,"—wins the day,

'Tis Taylor's to chase them in utter dismay.
Routed, beaten and stricken, Santa Anna retreats,
Unequal for Taylor, who knows no defeats.
Endeared to the nation; when peace is secured,

Modest hero, great general, to hardships inured,
A call now receives to the President's chair.
Noble in peace,—was as dauntless in war.

More unlikely for President none could be,
In means, his poor father—scarce any had he.
Little chance to get knowledge for him did appear,
Learning a luxury, and books they were dear.
At the age of fifteen had scarce read a book;
Ready for college—the poor youth ne'er did look.
Duly counseled by parents, to a clothier's trade

Fillmore is sent to learn how garments are made.
In the town of Sempronius he first gets a chance,
Library free, every mind may advance.
Like a wayfaring man who is hungry for food,
Millard sought out each book, read all that was good.
On every occasion he read when he could,
Reading and studying as not many would.
Every leisure hour spent in storing his mind.

Storing up knowledge he was wholly inclined.
Unbroken, four years he spent in this way,
Meets in with Judge Wood—oh most fortunate day!
More esteem'd than the Judge was not to be found,
Esteem'd by all classes the country around.
Rough in exterior the apprentice boy seem'd,

Hiding under this roughness what this gentleman deem'd
Intellectual resources, which only to shine,
Like the diamond, or jaspar, or ore from the mine,
Laid on them, requir'd but the artisan's hand,

Creating him polished, forever to stand.
A hint was sufficient—the youth was advised—
Young Fillmore to study, his talents devised.
Untiringly bends to the study of law,
Gives teaching a trial, at surveying, no daw.
Admitted at length to the bar he succeeds,

23

Carries the state, and soon he proceeds
On to the State House—signalizes his name,
Unlocks prison doors for poor debtors in shame.
Next to Congress elected, fills a term of two years,
Then to Buffalo returns, as a lawyer appears.
Yet again twice elected to Congress to go,

Next Governor made, for New York decides so.
Elected Comptroller, directs business and trade,
Within less than a year Vice-President made.

You may search all the pages of History o'er,
Of one you can't read, your regard merits more.
Rising from nothing, reaches higher his fame,
Keeping on till he won the President's name.

OTHER FAMOUS SUBJECTS

While numerous acrostics focus on British and American heads of state, many others portray a variety of famous subjects. The plurality of selections in this chapter pay homage to renowned writers. Others address an emperor, an explorer, a Founding Father, a general, a painter, and a scientist.

The crown jewel is five selections from Charles Vaughan Grinfield's *A Century of Acrostics on the Most Eminent Names in Literature, Science, and Art, Down to the Present Time* (1855). He noted that this might be the "first series" of acrostic poems to be published together as a book, and aside from two earlier works about monarchs, that appears to be the case. Grinfield explained that he composed the acrostics "to relieve some of the many unoccupied hours" he faced while suffering from "that greatest of afflictions, the deprivation of sight."

The acrostic castigating Benedict Arnold, a traitor to the Continental Army in the Revolutionary War, was written by his uncle, Oliver Arnold. The elder Arnold was a patriot and a frequent poet, and he loathed his nephew's treachery.

John Anketell

Sublimely great, the philosophic mind
In *Newton* shines, unequall'd, unconfin'd.
Regions and causes in dark chaos lost,
In his solutions clearest lustre boast.
Sunk in obscurity, of proof bereft,
Astronomy to errors maze was left;
At *Newton*'s call, uncertainty withdrew,
Conviction spoke, and wisdom rose to view:
No more the mist of ignorance prevails,
Enlighten'd truth its pleasing form reveals.
With rev'rend wonder, and supreme delight,
The whole creation opens to our sight.
Orb upon orb, in awful order plac'd,
Newton explor'd, and all their motions trac'd.

John Anketell

With boundless force the senses to command,
Immortal *Shakespeare* shall unrivall'd stand.
"Life's many color'd scenes" he boldly drew,
Look'd thro' the soul, and ev'ry passion knew.
Inventive beauties in his writing shine,
Acknowledg'd wit, and energy divine.
Mute tho' his tongue, to ruthless death a prey,
Still shall the poet transports sweet convey.
Harmonious numbers swell the melting strain,
As tender maidens breathe their love-sick pain:
Kindly affectionate the verses flow,
Expressing friends or parents' bliss or woe:
Strong rush the measures which in colors bright
Paint anger, jealousy, or mortal fight.
Enrich'd with elegance of style sublime,
Admiring crowds, in ev'ry peopled clime,
Resound his merit, and with candour own,
England's sweet bard all other bards outshone.

Chaucer

CHARLES VAUGHAN GRINFIELD

Chieftain and Father of our poet band,
How nobly dost thou take the foremost stand!
Amid thy "Pilgrims" picturesquely wild,
Uttering pure streams of "English undefil'd,"
Choice scenes of humourous life, antiquely quaint,
Each character life-like, not feebly faint,
Racy, fresh, vigourous, 'twas thine to paint.

Dante

CHARLES VAUGHAN GRINFIELD

Daring thy genius! mighty though it be
Amid the "Inferno" such dread scenes to see,
Nobly, yet simply, thy great task is wrought;
Thy "Comedy Divine" with grandeur fraught
E'en light from mediæval darkness brought.

Napoleon

CHARLES VAUGHAN GRINFIELD

Nations have rued the day when thou wast born,
Ambition was thy God—mad lust of power:
Pride, heartless selfishness, and cynic scorn,
O'er thee held sway, and were thy hateful dower.
Like the dread lion springing on his prey,
Empires to thee were things to o'erwhelm at will.
Oh, were it not for Waterloo's great day,
Not e'en, perchance, had ceas'd that thirst of conquest still.

Raphael

CHARLES VAUGHAN GRINFIELD

Regal thy rank among that Painter band,
All, the proud sons of fair Italia's land;
Pictures inspir'd by sacred themes are thine;
How nobly do thy great "Cartoons" outshine
All else, in grand and wonderful design:
Exalted title thus to thee is given,
Like what thou wrought'st "Divine," as caught from Heaven.

Tennyson

CHARLES VAUGHAN GRINFIELD

Thy verse is like rich music to the ear;
Elegant, tender, sweet, thy varied lays:
Now, soft as lute, or as the clarion clear,
Now, pensive as some song of olden days.
Young fancy revels in thy poet dreams,
Steep'd in such melody of words as none
Of elder laureate bards have pour'd—it seems
Now, like Æolian strains from breezy zephyrs won.

Christopher Columbus

Robert Blackwell

Commissioned by the king of Spain
He did a fleet of ships prepare;
Rejoicing, westward he set sail
In search of land he knew not where.
Some asserted he would find
The ocean deep, a boundless main;
Others, by sailing west it would
Prevent his coming back again.
Hopeful still he kept his course,
Ere long out glorious land he sees,
Rich, and covered o'er with trees.

Confirmed in what he thought was true,
Our lovely land he bids farewell;
Leaving this with joy he went
Unto his own the news to tell.
Men soon flocked here from every clime,
Both young and old, the rich and poor,
Until we see this happy land
Scattered now with cities o'er.

Patrick Henry

Robert Blackwell

Prior to the first war he lived in our land,
And was the foremost of all to take a bold stand
To oppose oppression; and the first that we see
Resolving to die or from Britain be free.
In our defense his speeches we hear;
Coming from one with vision so clear,
King George was made to tremble and fear.

He labored and struggled to set us all free,
Exclaiming, Give freedom or death unto me,
Naught else will serve my purpose, said he.
Resolving thus, in the sequel we read,
Young and old from fetters were freed.

C. A. M'Naughton

Cliosophic genius! though he is no more,
How many are the minds that yet can be
Amused, instructed, by his labours past!
Rare gift was his, for he had power to draw
Life's every type of character, and well
Each one was drawn. By rich and poor revered,
Still will his name live on, though he be dead.

Drawn from his "Christinas Books" have lessons been;
In each we find "moral adorn a tale."
Can we read trials of "Jo" or "Copperfield,"
Kind-hearted "Nickleby," poor forlorn "Smike,"
Endearing "Nell," but heart's best sympathy
New chords of pity feel for human woe?
Smiles suit thee best, not tears?—to "Pickwick" go.

Oliver Arnold

Born for a curse to virtue and mankind
Earth's broadest realm ne'er knew so black a mind,
Night's sable veil your crime can never hide
Each one so great t'would glut historic tide,
Defunct your cursed memory will live
In all the glare that infamy can give
Curses of all ages will attend your name
Traitors alone will glory in your shame.

Almighty vengeance sternly waits to roll
Rivers of sulphur on your treacherous soul
Nature looks shuddering back with conscious dread
On such a tarnished blot as she has made,
Let hell receive you, riveted in chains
Doomed to the hottest focus of its flames.

RELIGION

A tremendous amount of poetry is religious in nature. Religion and poetry "both spring from the same source," declared James Dalton Morrison in *Masterpieces of Religious Verse*. He explained that "poetry seems to have had its beginning as the handmaiden of religion." He added, "True religion and great poetry both deal with reality and touch life on its highest and its deepest levels."

The selections in this chapter address a range of religious subjects, including Christmas Day, eternity, Good Friday, original sin, philanthropy, vegetarianism, and yearning for Jesus Christ.

In *Mansions of the Skies* (1875), W. P. Chilton ambitiously spells out the entire Lord's Prayer with forty rhyming, seven-line stanzas. As if he were not working with enough constraints, Chilton even sneaks in his name—diagonally in italics—in stanza VIII. The longest acrostic in this volume, *Mansions of the Skies* mostly adheres to a narrative despite addressing varied religious teachings. "If some of the interesting and leading events of the Bible have been successfully interwoven with the devotional prayer of our Saviour, the result should rather be commended, than the execution of the plan rigidly criticised," Chilton explained in the poem's preface. "The author is aware of the difficulty of embracing a subject so comprehensive, in a space so limited, and of adjusting a poetic sentiment to an acrostic form so elaborate." Chilton also composed *Columbia* (1880), a lengthy acrostic spelling out the name of every state in the US.

While this chapter has a Christian focus, acrostics can be found in Judaism and Islam as well. Alphabet poems appear in the Bible and the Dead Sea Scrolls. Later Jewish poets embraced acrostics, and Jewish tombstones sometimes feature acrostic epitaphs in Hebrew. An Arabic alphabet poem praising the Muslim prophet Muhammad was written in Egypt in 1278.

On Original Sin

A Tradesman in Norfolk

O Thou foul spirit, that cou'd not be at rest,
Rov'd round the world to spoil man's happiness,
In words deceitful, yet so soft and fair,
Gain'd the attention of this happy pair;
Instant they took the fruit, they eat, they fell,
No longer now in paradise must dwell.
Alas! poor man is fallen very low,
Like to the beasts, his God he doth not know.

Sin is so twisted in the human nature,
In ev'ry part man is become a traitor,
Nor spurns at none so much as his Creator.

The Seeking Sinner

T. R.

"As the hart panteth after the water brooks, so panteth my soul
after Thee, O God: my soul thirsteth for God, for the living God,
when shall I come and appear before God." —Psalm XLII, 1–2

Precious Jehovah Jesus, heavenly Lord;
Author of Peace, revealed in Thy word:
Ne'er hath Thine ear of Grace refused to hear,
The cries of those, who seek Thy face in pray'r.
I come my Lord, and ask Thee for Thy Grace,
Nor can I comfort find, but as Thy face
Grants me a smile, and hid me *go in peace*.

Fully convinced that I a sinner am,
On Thee I trust, Thou Sin atoning Lamb,
Receive me Lord, and I will praise Thy Name.

Cause me to hear Thy soul elating voice,
Help Lord, *the bones, Thou'st broken, to rejoice,*
Rock of Eternal Ages, bid my soul
In Thee find rest, on Thee the burden roll.
Saviour of sinners, hear a sinner's cry,
Thy suppliant save, and bring Thy mercy nigh.

JOHN YEWDALL

Everlasting is my name;
Time upon me has no claim;
Evermore I shall endure;
Reader, now thy home secure;
Now, thy precious moments prize,
Into God's own image rise;
Then thou shalt in me be blest;
Yea, thou shalt in me find rest.

Philanthropy

JOHN YEWDALL

Philanthropy thou heaven-born guest,
How shall thy nature be exprest?
Inclin'd to seek for scenes of woe:
Loving thy goodness to bestow:
A father to the fatherless,
Near to the widow in distress;
Tender, beneficent, and kind,
Healing diseases of the mind:
Ready and willing to relieve
On all occasions—those who grieve.
Perfect in Christian charity;
Yes! such is true philanthropy.

Christmas Day

GEORGE WEST

Come friends, and all hail the return of this morn,
How lovely to think that a Saviour was born;
Rejoicing to meet where that Saviour will be,
Instead of where wicked rejoicings we see.
Say not with the drunkard, 'tis right to rejoice,
Take conscience to guide—attend that small voice;
Meet then with God's people on this happy day,
And join in that solemn assembly to pray;
Stay there, and ascending your thoughts far above,

Draw near and partake of that feast of His love,
And strive on this night to be able to say,
Yea, I have rejoic'd with my Saviour this day.

Good Friday

GEORGE WEST

Good Friday, 'tis call'd, and well may it be;
O think of Christ's goodness to you and to me;
O think how He there upon Calvary's tree
Died to save all from death, who saved will be,

Found His grave with the wicked, descended to hell,
Rose on the third day in glory to dwell,
Incarnate He sits at His Father's right hand.
Draw near and let's join His heavenly band:
And may we through that vast eternity sing;
Yield our praises to Him who salvation did bring.

Vegetarian Life: Sonnet Acrostic

WILLIAM EDWARD ARMYTAGE AXON

"They shall not kill in all my holy mountain,
saith the Lord." —Isaiah

Vision prophetic that Isaiah saw,
Earth had no brighter, fairer sight to show;
Guiltless of blood and innocent of woe,
Ever was rule of love the ample law.
They did not slay in all the holy mount,
All gentle life was sacred and was free—
Ranged in the air and sported in the sea—
In man and brute they saw life's common fount,
And in a chain of love bound all below,
Nor child nor lamb lacked a caressing hand.

Let us, then, make that holy mountain grow—
Isaiah's vision of the righteous land,—
Free from all tyrant force, by blood unstained,
Eden once more! Lo! Paradise regained.

Mansions of the Skies

W. P. CHILTON

The Lord's Prayer

I.

O Sweet, celestial Home—yon gilded sky—
Undimmed in radiance for endless years,
Robed bright in beauty for eternity!
Fain would I sing the Bliss which there appears,
Away from life's unceasing cares and tears;
The Peace which lasting springs in that abode—
Home ever blest—where sin nor cares corrode!

II.

Each raptured glance of the unclouded eye
Revealeth beauty in that realm above,
Where shining orbs in fadeless splendor vie,
Harmonious round their radiant centre move,
Obedient to the sure behests of love;
All joined with music of the spheres, in time
Roll on, in pure accord and sacred chime.

III.

Thou spirit that the bright seraphic throng
Inspirest with accent sweet, and gladsome praise,
Now lend thine aid enchanting; may my song
Heaven's poesy portray in beauteous lays,
Enrapt by blissful dream of halcyon days;
All vain must be, save with thy sacred fire,
Vain else I'd now invoke my humble lyre.

IV.

Enkindle new, thy bright, angelic flame,
Nor cease to linger near while I portray,
How man, in his creation pure, and aim,
And Godlike image made, tho' human way,
Lost the bright joys of Eden's blissful day;
Lost his high stale, and was condemned to roam
O'er the wide world, far from his peaceful home:

V.

When from the beauteous scenes of Paradise
'Driven, he moved in penitence and pain
Before his Maker; no resplendent prize
Enrapturing him, nor cheering hope to gain
The joys of Eden; till in heavenly strain
His soul is quickened, by the voice which gave
Young Hope to cheer, while journeying to the grave.

VI.

Nor cheers more sweetly than the Elysian goal
Awaiting the redeemed, beyond the grave—
Mansion of rest—where dwells the sinless soul,
Enraptured evermore, with him who gave
This beauteous land of bliss, this power to save.
Hope fondly points to that mysterious plan,
Yon pearly realm and blissful home for man.

VII.

Knowledge seraphic, there alone can pry
Into Empyrean splendors beaming far,
Never appearing to the finite eye;
God is the gracious giver; no rude jar
Doth seem along those giddy heights; but star
O'er star revolving, each at his command,
Makes sure the glory of that better land.

VIII.

Can man, so frail a creature of the dust,
O'ercast here by the great celestial sphere
Made by the skill inspired, that doth adjust
Each world of varying light—can man declare
There's no Creator of these works so fair?
How grandly speak the brilliant orbs which span
Yon spacious realm, that God alone doth scan?

IX.

Who is this God! whence sprang this mighty power,
Infused in all created realms and space,
Leaving its print on every tree and flower,
Lingering on nature's ever-varied face,
Bearing, along with beauty, matchless grace,
Enlivening sweet our homeward journey on,
Doth plainly seem to Deity alone.

X.

On yon bright pearly home and seraph land
No blemish doth appear; and angels trace
Each work perfected by the skilful hand
Of Providence; tho' sin did once embrace
No meagre part of that celestial place,
Embittering Heaven's peace and holy love,
And rousing the angelic hosts above.

XI.

Round the Majestic Throne sin could not dwell!
The great angelic throng poured forth, as one
Heaven-inspired, the Godlike Michael
Against the embattled hosts of Abaddon,
Swiftly to meet Heaven's now rebellious son.
In countless throngs the seraphs soon proclaim
The cause triumphant in Jehovah's name.

XII.

In conclave holy, was a just decree,
Sending the dragon hence that blest abode;
In chains of terror, he was loath to see
New evil, which his damning guilt forebode;
Heavenward he gazed, in dire, revengeful mood;
E'en hope has vanished, and profound despair
Awakes his soul, in dismal musing there.

XIII.

Vainly these restless, banished spirits seek,
E'en yet, the will of Heaven to oppose;
No gladding words the cheerless ones could speak,
Grieving that their celestial reign must close;
In vain they writhe, and dare to interpose;
Vainly they seek to change the dire command,
E'er driving them from the bright heavenly land.

XIV.

United in the bonds of holy love,
Seraphic praise now blends with joy unfeigned,
That discord, from the happy scenes above,
Had to Apollyon winged its way, and reigned
In distant realms, where hope ne'er more obtained:
Sweet contrast springs in joy and peaceful rest,
Dwelling in sinless regions of the blessed.

XV.

Away from God's bright realm the dragon turned—
Yet pined he for the glory of command
On high; deep thirst for power within him burned:
Unnumbered schemes to repossess that land
Renewed his strength and his despairing band;
Defeated still, in each fond hope to reign,
Ambition leads him other worlds to gain.

XVI.

In darkness deep, and wild despair now chained,
Lingered no hope within his guilty breast;
Yet potent still for wrong, he ne'er refrained—
Because of his dire ruin—to arrest
Reason's fell sway, which made him so oppressed:
Each aim was his, and sought this end alone—
Against his God, to rear his dismal throne.

XVII.

Dwelling in sullen grandeur, now supreme
Among the fallen angel spirits there;
Ne'er ceasing, as a wild, impetuous stream,
Dashing its raging current far and near,
Fiercely to war 'gainst all to Heaven dear;
O'er fairest fields his emissaries move,
Resolved against the beauteous land of love.

XVIII.

God fashioned now the earth, by sweet command,
In form and beauty peerless; and by word
Vision of wonders gave, that o'er the land
Each day were formed—fair handwork of the Lord—
Unrivalled wisdom of the Triune God!
Six days in all, creation He could span,
On seventh He rested, and gave this man.

XIX.

Upon this new-made orb, a paradise,
Redolent with odors sweet from flowery vale,
That bore the impress of the bending skies,
Receiving loveliness, which did regale
Each tree and meadow, shrub and blossom frail;
Shone forth a peaceful home, with joys replete,
Perchance, where love the soul would ever greet.

XX.

Amid this blissful scene and wondrous frame—
Sweet home of gladness and of works so fair—
Satan, in Eden comes, with artful name,
Enticing Eve, of matchless beauty there;
Smoothly he speaks, and fills her soul with care.
All his vile counsels, veiled in deep disguise,
Seem thus to shine in livery of the skies.

XXI.

When evening's shade its mantle threw o'er day—
Ere nightfall—Adam moved 'mong favored bowers
Forlorn, with saddened heart, oppressed: no ray
Of hope was his, nor cheer from earth's sweet flowers;
Rest came ne'er more, but long and weary hours.
God's mercy still prevailed, as he did move,
In silence pure, along the trembling grove.

XXII.

Voice of Jehovah! dread commanding tone!
Eden's fair plains are filled with awe profound,
To hear the sentence from the sovereign throne,
Harrowing the soul in dark transgression found.
On the vile serpent Eve's first sins rebound;
So Adam, by Eve's siren voice so sweet
Entranced, the long-forbidden fruit did eat.

XXIII.

Where now is hope in Eden's beauteous plan?
Has reason yielded now to fell despair?
Oh no! God a dear promise gives to man:
The only Son, who made the earth so fair—
Redeemer of mankind—descends to hear,
E'en on His soul so pure, the sinner's blame,
Sin to atone, and share the culprit's shame.

XXIV.

Pure paradise on earth no more could be
A joyous home for man—but lost estate;
Sorrow and toil was now Heaven's just decree,
Subscribed and sealed, which angels thus relate,
As Cherubim attest the saddened fate.
God, pitying them, a cheering hope doth lend,
As the grieved pair their dismal way descend.

41

XXV.

Inspired with hope new Paradise to gain,
Now promised of the bright celestial land,
Sweet incense, blent with music's charming strain,
To Heaven ascends; and there with seraphs' band,
United song, resounds the golden strand:
Sweetly the answering spirit fills the soul
Anew with hope of the celestial goal.

XXVI.

New hope and love, with Abel's incense pure,
Dawn brightly now, and point to climes of rest,
Lustrous with glory always to endure,
Enriched with treasure of divine bequest—
A peaceful, happy home, forever blest.
Down from the golden realm—the Great White Throne—
Unmingled rays of mercy, lingering, shone.

XXVII.

Sweet spirit! from thy lofty sphere serene,
Now linger o'er this heart communion pure,
Of man and Creator; this gloried scene,
That wakes in ecstasy the soul, secure
In its bright realm, where sin can ne'er allure:
Ne'er sweeter chime along Heaven's Archway ran,
Than welcomed this blest gift of hope to man.

XXVIII.

Over the land, in rapid course of time,
The vilest sins prevailed, in deed and aim;
Evil imaginings, that lead to crime,
Making Jehovah grieve that He could claim,
Perchance, few subjects loyal to His name:
Tho' Enoch, faithful, walked in peace with God,
And righteous Noah escaped the mighty flood.

XXIX.

This humble seer a warning voice did raise,
In pity for the souls of men defiled;
Over the land, foretelling woful days—
Nor did they cease from sin, but e'en reviled,
Because of unbelief, which them beguiled;
Until the pangs of deep remorse unfold
The saddened fate the messenger foretold.

XXX.

Deriding once, these men the world would give
Even the face to see—long laughed to scorn.
Lingered with them a hope, tho' faint, to live;
In vain they cry, and bitterly they mourn;
Vainly now wish that man had ne'er been born.
Ere long the wrathful torrents of the sky
Rush o'er the plains, and shroud the mountains high!

XXXI.

Unseen, bright seraphs weep the dreadful fall.
Sweetly there spans the curtain of the sky—
Fair charming sight—the bow of promise; all,
Regaled in matchless beauty for the eye
Of man—a shining covenant on high—
Measuring with gorgeous arch both land and sea,
E'en gilds all nature's choice and verdant lea.

XXXII.

Viewing the token beautiful, that gleams
In brilliant colors o'er the expanse of blue;
Love springs forth freely as the gushing streams
Flowing thro' flowery lea of varying hue,
O'er fairest fields, refreshing each anew;
Rekindled hope awakes in every breast,
That all mankind through Abram shall be blessed.

XXXIII.

How merciful, O God! Thou art to man
In all Thy ways! how bountiful in grace!
Ne'er failing, as in Israel's chosen plan—
Egypt's fair land, when fled, and Pharaoh's face—
In timely gifts, thy sons, thy love could trace;
So, as we journey to the promised land,
Thy loving grace we seek, and guiding hand.

XXXIV.

Hope gleams more brightly with each fleeting year,
Ere long to see, as taught in prophecy,
King of the world, Messiah, now appear
In power, yet love and sacred majesty;
Ne'er more to yield His royal sceptred sway;
Go forth in meekness, rightfully to claim,
Dominion true, in His loved Father's name.

XXXV.

O sure prophetic token, star divine!
Magi and angels greet thee in the skies—
As the bright herald and celestial sign,
Near lingers where the holy infant lies,
Dazzling the sight in glad tho' strange surprise.
Through boundless realms the joyous tidings ring,
Hailing the advent of Immanuel, King.

XXXVI.

Ere long the power of Deity is seen
Perfected, in Messiah's human form;
Oh! blending pure of Heaven in nature's mien,
Wherein is strength to quell the raging storm;
E'en power the troubled waters to transform;
Relief bestows by all atoning grace,
And death makes joy in Jesus' shining face.

XXXVII.

Nor was Immanuel, Prince, from sorrow free.
Descended He from Heaven, for sacrifice;
The bitter cup of dark Gethsemane
He drank; then turned in love His tearful eyes
E'en to His Father, and for mercy cries!
Great tho' His grief and mental agony,
Love crowns His brow with royal majesty.

XXXVIII.

On the accursed tree our Saviour hangs!
Racked is his soul with anguish and with pain!
Yon Heaven grows black with anger o'er His pangs,
Frowning to see the Lamb of God now slain!
O'er Him bright angels bend in lengthened train;
Rent is the veil, while God's anointed dies!
Earth quakes with fear, and martyred saints arise!

XXXIX.

Verily, now, the Son of God is slain!
E'en from the sombre portals of the grave,
Rekindled love inspires the seraph train
Away the stone to roll; and Heaven gave
New power to Him, who fallen man did save.
Despised He was, still Mary Magdalene
E'en lingers where His body once had lain.

XL.

Visions of fadeless light beyond the skies
Enrapture Him, wreathed in immortal peace;
Rests He on earth, save as few kindred ties
Awake His soul to sweet communion's bliss.
Majestic risen from His dark decease,
Eternal glory on His way attends!
Now his joyed spirit with the Father blends.

NATURE

"The natural world has been one of the recurring subjects of poetry, frequently the primary one, in every age and country," observed Edward Hirsch in *The Essential Poet's Glossary*.

Nature takes many forms. Subjects in this chapter encompass a plant, a flower, an Australian flower show, an American national park, and celestial bodies. The eclectic source material includes *Pipe and Pouch: The Smoker's Own Book of Poetry*, an anthology that glorifies smoking, and *Acrostic Sonnets and Other Poems*, which primarily features acrostic sonnets. The three-line verse about the sun is the shortest selection in this volume.

An Acrostic Sonnet to Yosemite Valley

J. E. O'CONNOR

Ye Tow'ring Cliffs and Ye Far-Falling Streams!
O Valley of the Gods, Thou Wonderland,
Shaped by the Mighty Sculptor's master hand,
Excelling all man's most colossal schemes!
Mute, overawed, to me once more it seems
I stand upon exalted glacier and,
Transfixt by Thy stupendous glories grand,
Enraptured gaze, thrilled by a thousand themes.

Vernal the exquisite, unrivalled, queen,
Ahwahnee guarded by the Sentinel,
Lake, mirror of Thy grandeur, calm, serene,
Like Bridal's mist across my mem'ry float.
Enchanted Vale, still haunts my soul Thy spell,
Yosemite, like some great organ's note.

An Acrostic on the Primrose

J. QUESTED

Pale peeping from its leafy root,
Rob'd in the richest green,
Its fragrant odour all its fruit,
Morn's fav'rite flow'r is seen.
Regaling is the scent it spreads
O'er the expanded vale;
Sequester'd lie its lowly beds,
Enriching ev'ry gale.

47

C. A. M'Naughton

Cull choicest, brightest blooms
Out of your gardens gay;
Luxuriantly sweet Flora's gifts
Let us display to-day;
Indictive is our right
Now proudly here to show
Garlands fair, plants most rare,
Which in our city grow.
O trust we that great good
Out of this cause will spring—
Displaying Nature's works to man
    Must God to man's mind bring.

Fair flowers! ye can teach
Life's lesson to us all;
Our lives are like your own—
We live but for to fall!
Each human life is even like to thine—
Remains to work God's will, then fades from time.

Success to Collingwood, and to its Show!
H. Walker long be spared the same to know!
Owe we most thanks to him that we can boast
Within our city this an annual toast:
    "Collingwood Flower Show!"

J. H.

To thee, blest weed, whose sovereign wiles,
O'er cankered care bring radiant smiles,
Best gift of Love to mortals given!
At once the bud and bliss of Heaven!
Crownless are kings uncrowned by thee;
Content the serf in thy sweet liberty,
O charm of life! O foe to misery!

Sun

ROBERT BLACKWELL

Source of heat and source of light,
Upholding by thy strength and might
Numerous seas and planets bright.

Moon

ROBERT BLACKWELL

Mounted far above the sky,
Onward rolling, tell us why
Our eyes they can not see
No sweet and lovely stream on thee.

Stars

ROBERT BLACKWELL

Seen through no glass, to the naked eye
They look like gems set in the sky;
And yet they are but planets high,
Revolving round ten thousand suns,
Swift, yet smooth as water runs.

MISCELLANY

Although many acrostics fit into the preceding categories, quite a few do not. The form is adaptable in various directions, beyond addressing people's names and the most common poetic themes.

Robert Blackwell's acrostics about California, cars, and fame were published in 1868. The California verse appeared two decades after the state's gold rush started. The poem about cars refers to railcars—four decades after construction began on the first American railroad and eighteen years before the first automobile was patented.

Half of the selections in this chapter mention God without having an overarching religious focus, showing how faith permeates myriad areas of life. It can be difficult to determine where to draw the line for which poems qualify as religious. Sophie A. M. James's acrostic sonnet with New Year well-wishing uses some religious language, and it appeared in her poetry collection titled *God's Answer, and Other Poems* (1880).

In an anthology championing poems taken from eclectic sources, the final two selections are among the most unexpected. An inmate spelled out Massachusetts State Prison in *Voices from Prison* (1849). The poet laureate of England's oldest golf club penned an acrostic about the organization and recited it at a club dinner in 1866. The verse was included in his 1873 book of poetry about the club, which was distributed to members.

California

ROBERT BLACKWELL

Country far renowned for gold,
And for soil, rich and new,
Lofty hills and torrents bold,
Immense streams, and branches too,
Flow through thy hills of old.
O happy land, illustrious one,
Richest, brightest clime that be,
No land, no State beneath the sun,
In all God's wide dominion free,
Acquires wealth so fast as thee.

Cars

ROBERT BLACKWELL

Clatter, clatter, here they come,
A wondrous source of power,
Running at a rapid rate,
Some thirty miles per hour.

Fame

ROBERT BLACKWELL

From what I see, some seek for thee,
As something worthy greeting;
Missing their aim, they thee proclaim
Elusive, worthless, fleeting.

Acrostic—Sonnet

SOPHIE A. M. JAMES

A bright new year to thee and thine, dear friend,
Bright in the highest sense the word can mean.
Receive these loving lines that now I send,
In token of my feelings warm and keen.
God knows I wish thee ev'ry happiness.
Heaven strew flowers on thy earthly way,
Turning for thee all darkness into day.
Nor ever think that I can love thee less,
Each year I seem to prize thee more and more,
Words fail to tell how deep my friendship is;
Yet I would wish thee more than human bliss,
Earth's joys last not, its pleasures soon are o'er.
A prayer I'd breathe—life done—may God in love
Reach forth His hand, and take thee home above!

C. M.

Men—the poor despised ones of our fallen race,
Are cooped within these gloomy granite towers;
Summers and winters pass with creeping pace,
Seasons have no change—Spring time hath no flowers,
Autumn, once so loved, so balmy and serene,
Comes cheerless now to these poor, sorrowing eyes.
Heavenly orbits course their glittering paths unseen,
Unseen are those bright gems whose beauty fills the skies.
Sleepless nights and joyless days here go and come;
Evenings or mornings bring no cheering ray;
There's no endearing welcome to a happy home;
There's nought to crown the labors of the day.
Stranger,—whoe'er thou be, or whatsoe'er thou art,
Sure thou with kindly words can pity show,—
'Twould bring a warmer feeling to the chilled heart,
And raise a hope where all is hopeless now.
These poor despised ones all have hearts like thee;
Each one can feel the cheering power of love.
Perchance thou might with words of sympathy
Raise their stray thoughts to better things above.
If they have fallen in temptation's snare,
Still they have kindred claims which God has given;
Oh! lead them back with kindly words, and spare
No tones of love, but cheer them on to heaven.

Round this old table we once more are seated,
On match-making now our hearts are all bent;
Youthful aspirants—although perhaps defeated—
At retrieving lost laurels we know are intent.
Lemons and sugar with whisky so mellow,
Business with pleasure, this night we combine.
Lots of matches the captain will book to each fellow;
All the more matches made, why, all the more wine;
Clearly you see then that these little dinners
Kindle fresh friendships and old ones renew,
Holding together both losers and winners—
Each game that you've played you can calmly review.
As in Golf, so in life, you most surely will find it—
Together the rough with the smooth will be found;
Here a piece of fine turf—but a *bunker* behind it—
Good Golfing is that which gets over the ground.
Of all games that are played 'tis far the most pleasant;
Long have I known it, yet hope to know more;
Full surely my notions are shared by all present;
Come, three cheers for the old game that we all adore;
Long may we live, and ne'er may we sever—
Untarnished our name for ever we'll fix—
Brightly this club's shone; may it flourish for ever!

GEORGE MOSES HORTON

George Moses Horton (ca. 1797–ca. 1883) was born into slavery. During his late teens, he began peddling produce to students at the University of North Carolina at Chapel Hill. He soon transitioned to selling acrostics and other love poems for $0.25 to $0.75 each. Unable to write until around 1832, Horton composed the poems in his head while handling a plow during the week and dictated them to students on Sundays. Undergraduates purchased the poems and sent them to their girlfriends back home—"the tip-top belles of Virginia, South Carolina, and Georgia," as Horton put it. When he was able to pay his master $0.50 a day, Horton gave up farmwork and focused on being a professional poet.

Legend has it that James K. Polk, the future president, was the first student to encourage Horton. One patron was Sion Hart Rogers, who became a Confederate lieutenant and the attorney general of North Carolina. In 1865, Union soldiers commissioned Horton to write acrostics about their sweethearts.

In *The Black Bard of North Carolina*, Joan R. Sherman showed why Horton was such a groundbreaking figure: "Horton was the first American slave to protest his bondage in verse; the first African American to publish a book in the South; the only slave to earn a significant income by selling his poems; the only poet of any race to produce a book of poems *before* he could write; and the only slave to publish two volumes of poetry while in bondage and another shortly after emancipation."

Most of Horton's acrostics are not extant, as they were sent to far-flung recipients. The following selections are from roughly 1835 to 1854. Some are excerpted from longer poems that continued in the same rhyme scheme without the acrostic structure.

Joy, like the morning, breaks from one divine—
Unveiling streams which cannot fail to shine.
Long have I strove to magnify her name
Imperial, floating on the breeze of fame.

Attracting beauty must delight afford,
Sought of the world and of the Bards adored;
Her grace of form and heart-alluring powers
Express her more than fair, the queen of flowers.

Pleasure, fond nature's stream, from beauty sprung,
And was the softest strain the Muses sung,
Reverting sorrows into speechless Joys,
Dispelling gloom which human peace destroys.

For the Fair Miss M. M. McL

GEORGE MOSES HORTON

May this inspired acrostic prove
A perfect token of my love
Return thy torch almost expired
Yet find by whom thou art admired

My soul of love would fly to thee
Constrained thy winning form to see

Like Pan whose destiny was grief
Exploring nature for relief
And sure when thee my love has found
Nought else in life can heal the wound

Mistress of green in flowers arrayed
Alluring all my heart away
Replete with glory not to fade
Yet flourish in eternal May—
Eternalized by distant fame—
Void of a shade in bloom divine—
Pleasures await thy sacred name
Or bid thee still proceeds to shine
Who has surpassed thy heavenly mien
Expression will forbear to tell
Like thee not one I yet have seen
Let all adore *thee* lovely belle

So let our names together blend
In floods of union to the end
Or flow together soul in soul
Nor distance break the soft control—
How pleasing is the thought to me
A thought of such a nymph as thee
Reverts my language into song
That flows delightful soft along—
Return to me a soft reply
On which I must with joy rely
Give me thy hand and then thy heart
Entirely mingled not to part
Relume the tapor near expired
Seeking a friend so long desired—

Inimitable Beauty

GEORGE MOSES HORTON

Selected lady belle of beauty blessed
Of course I laud thee far above the rest
Pleased with thy grace I can neglect thee never
How can I fail to sing of thee forever
I never never can the weight remove
And shut my eyes against the torch of love

A Lord may smile upon his flaunting train
Like seraphs marching o'er the Elysian plain
Extolling high his love inspiring host
Xerxes the mighty peer may sing and boast
And they fall short however famed divine
Nor can their beauty be compared to thine
Dispelling darkness as they brightly shine:
Eager I gaze as on a star above
Reflecting light which kindles into love

EDGAR ALLAN POE

Although Edgar Allan Poe (1809–49) was chiefly revered for his fiction, he prided himself as a poet foremost. According to Thomas Ollive Mabbott, the editor of a complete collection of Poe's poems, "He began to be [a poet] in boyhood, and continued to write verse to the end of his life. His actual product is small, but the proportion of excellence is surprisingly high, and . . . his powers never waned; they increased."

Poe wrote a pair of acrostics spelling out the name of his cousin Elizabeth Rebecca Herring in her album circa 1829. Albums were books where family, friends, and acquaintances could share autographs and personalized messages, sometimes including poetry and art.

Poe penned two diagonal acrostics, using the first letter of the first line, the second letter of the second line, etc. "A Valentine" (1846) and "An Enigma" (1847) spell out the names of a fellow poet and a patron, respectively. Because the names are hidden, the poems are enigmas, or riddles in verse. "An Enigma" is also a sonnet. Arranging a name diagonally while adhering to the fixed parameters of a sonnet is significantly more challenging than composing a standard acrostic.

Elizabeth

EDGAR ALLAN POE

Elizabeth—it surely is most fit
(Logic and common usage so commanding)
In thy own book that *first* thy name be writ,
Zeno and other sages notwithstanding;
And *I* have other reasons for so doing
Besides my innate love of contradiction;
Each poet—*if* a poet—in pursuing
The muses thro' their bowers of Truth or Fiction,
Has studied very little of his part,
Read nothing, written less—in short's a fool
Endued with neither soul, nor sense, nor art,
Being ignorant of one important rule,
Employed in even the theses of the school—
Called—I forget the heathenish Greek name—
(Called any thing, its meaning is the same)
"Always write *first* things uppermost in the heart."

A Valentine

EDGAR ALLAN POE

For her these lines are penned, whose luminous eyes,
Bright and expressive as the stars of Leda,
Shall find her own sweet name that, nestling, lies
Upon this page, enwrapped from every reader.
Search narrowly these words, which hold a treasure
Divine—a talisman, an amulet
That must be worn *at heart*. Search well the measure—
The words—the letters themselves. Do not forget
The smallest point, or you may lose your labor.
And yet there is in this no Gordian knot
Which one might not undo without a sabre
If one could merely understand the plot.
Upon the open page on which are peering
Such sweet eyes now, there lies, I say, *perdu*,
A musical name oft uttered in the hearing
Of poets, by poets—for the name is a poet's too.
In common sequence set, the letters lying,
Compose a sound delighting all to hear—
Ah, this you'd have no trouble in descrying
Were you not something, of a dunce, my dear—
And now I leave these riddles to their Seer.

An Enigma

Edgar Allan Poe

"Seldom we find," says Solomon Don Dunce,
　"Half an idea in the profoundest sonnet.
Through all the flimsy things we see at once
　As easily as through a Naples bonnet—
　Trash of all trash!—how *can* a lady don it?
Yet heavier far than your Petrarchan stuff—
Owl-downy nonsense that the faintest puff
　Twirls into trunk-paper the while you con it."
And, veritably, Sol is right enough.
The general tuckermanities are arrant
Bubbles—ephemeral and *so* transparent—
　But *this* is, now,—you may depend upon it—
Stable, opaque, immortal—all by dint
Of the dear names that lie concealed within 't.

LEWIS CARROLL

While Lewis Carroll (1832–98) is best known as the author of *Alice's Adventures in Wonderland* and its sequel, *Through the Looking-Glass*, he also wrote 150 poems, including nonsense verse, parodies, and more than a dozen acrostics. No other prominent writer has penned so many distinct works in the acrostic form. In *The Oxford Guide to Word Games*, Tony Augarde dubbed Carroll the "master of acrostics."

Most of Carroll's acrostics spell out the names of young girls he knew. While he composed some acrostics as inscriptions and in other obscure venues, he also featured them in several of his books. The most prominent example is at the end of *Through the Looking-Glass* (1871). Hailed as Carroll's best acrostic, it recalls the day that he started telling the Alice story to the three Liddell sisters, including Alice's namesake inspiration, Alice Pleasance Liddell. Other acrostics appear in *The Hunting of the Snark* (1876), *Sylvie and Bruno* (1889), and *Sylvie and Bruno Concluded* (1893).

In *The Mystery of Lewis Carroll*, Jenny Woolf explained that Carroll was "inspired by the limitations of the acrostic form" and that he "relished the task of creating more technically difficult acrostics, and some of these are very clever." Woolf noted that the restrictions "pushed him to write particularly well," perhaps because "he was concentrating on perfecting the technical form rather than on trying to push a message, thereby giving his usually-controlled unconscious thoughts an opportunity to see the light of day."

Several selections in this chapter demonstrate Carroll's next-level approach. In addition to spelling out the names Gertrude Chataway and Isa Bowman, those acrostics sound or spell out one syllable of the name at the beginning of each stanza. Two acrostics rely on dialogue. The final selection spells out a name using the third letter of each line. Carroll's ingenuity extended not just to standard acrostic poems but also acrostic puzzles, one of which has never been completely solved.

63

From *Through the Looking-Glass*

LEWIS CARROLL

A boat, beneath a sunny sky,
Lingering onward dreamily
In an evening of July—

Children three that nestle near,
Eager eye and willing ear,
Pleased a simple tale to hear—

Long has paled that sunny sky:
Echoes fade and memories die:
Autumn frosts have slain July.

Still she haunts me, phantomwise,
Alice moving under skies
Never seen by waking eyes.

Children yet, the tale to hear,
Eager eye and willing ear,
Lovingly shall nestle near.

In a Wonderland they lie,
Dreaming as the days go by,
Dreaming as the summers die:

Ever drifting down the stream—
Lingering in the golden gleam—
Life, what is it but a dream?

From *The Hunting of the Snark*

LEWIS CARROLL

Inscribed to a Dear Child:
In Memory of Golden Summer Hours and
Whispers of a Summer Sea

Girt with a boyish garb for boyish task,
Eager she wields her spade; yet loves as well
Rest on a friendly knee, intent to ask
The tale he loves to tell.

Rude spirits of the seething outer strife.
Unmeet to read her pure and simple spright,
Deem, if you list, such hours a waste of life,
Empty of all delight!

Chat on, sweet Maid, and rescue from annoy
Hearts that by wiser talk are unbeguiled.
Ah, happy he who owns that tenderest joy,
The heart-love of a child!

Away, fond thoughts, and vex my soul no more!
Work claims my wakeful nights, my busy days—
Albeit bright memories of that sunlit shore
Yet haunt my dreaming gaze!

"Are you deaf, Father William?" the young man said,
"Did you hear what I told you just now?
"Excuse me for shouting! Don't waggle your head
"Like a blundering, sleepy old cow!
"A little maid dwelling in Wallington Town,
"Is my friend, so I beg to remark:
"Do you think she'd be pleased if a book were sent down
"Entitled 'The Hunt of the Snark?'"

"Pack it up in brown paper!" the old man cried,
"And seal it with olive-and-dove.
"I command you to do it!" he added with pride,
"Nor forget, my good fellow, to send her beside
"Easter Greetings, and give her my love."

Love among the Roses

LEWIS CARROLL

"Seek ye Love, ye fairy-sprites?
    Ask where reddest roses grow.
  Rosy fancies he invites,
  And in roses he delights,
    Have ye found him?" "No!"

"Seek again, and find the boy
    In Childhood's heart, so pure and clear."
  Now the fairies leap for joy,
    Crying, "Love is here!"

"Love has found his proper nest;
    And we guard him while he dozes
  In a dream of peace and rest
    Rosier than roses."

LEWIS CARROLL

Around my lonely hearth, to-night,
   Ghostlike the shadows wander:
Now here, now there, a childish sprite,
Earthborn and yet as angel bright,
   Seems near me as I ponder.

Gaily she shouts: the laughing air
   Echoes her note of gladness—
Or bends herself with earnest care
Round fairy-fortress to prepare
Grim battlement or turret-stair—
   In childhood's merry madness!

New raptures still hath youth in store.
   Age may but fondly cherish
Half-faded memories of yore—
Up, craven heart! repine no more!
Love stretches hands from shore to shore:
   Love is, and shall not perish!

From *Sylvie and Bruno*

Lewis Carroll

Is all our Life, then, but a dream
Seen faintly in the golden gleam
Athwart Time's dark resistless stream?

Bowed to the earth with bitter woe,
Or laughing at some raree-show,
We flutter idly to and fro.

Man's little Day in haste we spend,
And, from its merry noontide, send
No glance to meet the silent end.

From *Sylvie and Bruno Concluded*

Lewis Carroll

Dreams, that elude the Walker's frenzied grasp—
Hands, stark and still, on a dead Mother's breast,
Which nevermore shall render clasp for clasp,
Or deftly soothe a weeping Child to rest—
In suchlike forms me listeth to portray
My Tale, here ended. Thou delicious Fay—
The guardian of a Sprite that lives to tease thee—
Loving in earnest, chiding but in play
The merry mocking Bruno! Who, that sees thee,
Can fail to love thee, Darling, even as I?—
My sweetest Sylvie, we must say "Good-bye!"

THREE PRESIDENTS AND A FIRST LADY

There is a rich tradition of honoring presidents with laudatory acrostics. Three presidents and a First Lady tried their hand at the form.

George Washington penned an unfinished acrostic to his teenage crush. The lines corresponding to the last four letters of her name, Frances Alexander, were not written. This acrostic is one of two poems that appeared in his diary in 1749–50.

Other than Jimmy Carter, John Quincy Adams is the only US president to write a book of poetry. The sixth president published an epic poem after he left the White House, and a collection of his shorter verse appeared posthumously. Adams wrote about 350 extant poems, including three acrostics. He wrote the selection in this chapter for the daughter of his colleague in Congress. In his diary, Adams complained that it was a "grievous miser[y]" to be "perpetually beset with albums and for autographs with a few lines of poetry," but he felt obliged after complying previously.

His wife, Louisa Catherine Adams, wrote at least four acrostics during her time as First Lady. Two praised Rep. Daniel Webster, a political ally, and one lambasted Sen. John Randolph, a rival. She later explained that Randolph's "temperament was irritable and sensitive almost to madness; and he was incessantly goaded on in his political career by a wild ambition, ill regulated passions, petty jealousies and indomitable perseverance."

At seventeen, Ulysses S. Grant wrote an acrostic spelling out the name of his sweetheart, Mary King, before attending the US Military Academy at West Point. The future Civil War hero explains that his "country calls" and he will "gain the field of glory."

The Washington and Grant poems are widely attributed to those presidents, but consensus about the authorship is not unanimous among scholars.

GEORGE WASHINGTON

From your bright sparkling Eyes, I was undone;
Rays, you have more transparent than the sun,
Amidst its glory in the rising Day,
None can you equal in your bright array;
Constant in your calm and unspotted Mind;
Equal to all, but will to none Prove kind,
So knowing, seldom one so Young, you'l Find
Ah! woe's me, that I should Love and conceal,
Long have I wish'd, but never dare reveal,
Even though severly Loves Pains I feel;
Xerxes that great, was't free from Cupids Dart,
And all the greatest Heroes, felt the smart.

JOHN QUINCY ADAMS

Mark the revolving seasons as they roll.
And let them teach instruction to thy soul.
Read and reflect—and thus shalt then ensure,
Youth's blooming bud and age's fruit mature.
Mark in thy progress o'er the stage of life
One scene of Folly, wickedness and strife
Refrain from earth's temptations as they rise
Refrain, and look to those beyond the skies
In calm composure, virtue's path pursue
Still to thyself and to thy maker true

What wou'd my feeble Muse so boldly fly?
Even aspire to a theme so high?
Bid her beware, to excellence so vast
She to attain can never hope at last.
'Tis Byron's pen alone this theme can share
Entwining judgement with discretion fair
Reason with learning; wit with talents rare.

Recipe for the Spleen, From an Old Woman

LOUISA CATHERINE ADAMS

Judgement I will not recommend
Of sense perhaps a grain, or two.
Have flights of fancy, *villipend*
Nor mind of *all* you say is true.

Read all the jest books thro' with care,
Abusive sarcasm prepare;
Nor wormwood scruple now to steep.
Dark hellebore and snake root deep,
Of malice take a heavy drachm
Let Envy there in mortar jam,
Pints of the gall you may infuse
Half of the dose take if you choose—

———

While venom from the tongue you spit
Tipsy, you'll think you've spoken Wit—

ULYSSES S. GRANT

My country calls and I obey,
And shortly I'll be on my way,
Removed from home far in the West,
Yet you with home and friends are blest.

Kindly then remember me.
I'll also often think of thee,
Nor forget the soldier story,
Gone to gain the field of glory.

POTPOURRI OF PROMINENT POETS

The poets in this chapter are known entities in poetic and literary circles, demonstrating that the acrostic form was embraced by revered bards. One selection is included from each poet.

John Keats was one of the leading English Romantic poets. Ben Jonson, a dramatist second only to William Shakespeare in his day, began his play *The Alchemist* with a prefatory acrostic. Robert Bridges and Thomas Jordan were poets laureate of England and London, respectively. Jane Johnston Schoolcraft, also called Bamewawagezhikaquay in the Ojibwa language, was the first known female Native American writer. Irish physicist John Tyndall explained why the sky is blue, and in one of his half-dozen acrostics, he discussed the "azure" and "cerulean" sky.

James Gates Percival and Nathaniel Parker Willis both penned acrostic sonnets spelling out the name of Emilie Marshall, whom the former identified as "a Boston lady of surpassing beauty." The preface of *American Sonnets*, which included both selections, dubbed Marshall "the reigning beauty of her day." The acrostic by Wilfrid Scawen Blunt is also a sonnet.

In the acrostic by George Herbert, the capitalized words spell out a quotation from the Letter of Paul to the Colossians, which is part of the New Testament. In the double acrostic by Jordan, the bold letters in crisscrossing diagonal lines spell out the names of two star-crossed lovers.

Acrostic–Sonnet

Nathaniel Parker Willis

Elegance floats about thee like a dress,
 Melting the airy motion of thy form
Into one swaying grace; and loveliness
 Like a rich tint that makes a picture warm
Is lurking in the chestnut of thy tress,
 Enriching it, as moonlight after storm

Mingles dark shadows into gentleness.
 A beauty that bewilders like a spell
Reigns in thine eye's clear hazel, and thy brow,
 So pure in vein'd transparency, doth tell
How spiritually beautiful art thou—
 A temple where angelic love might dwell.
Life in thy presence were a thing to keep,
Like a gay dreamer clinging to his sleep.

Sonnet

James Gates Percival

Earth holds no fairer, lovelier one than thou,
 Maid of the laughing lip, and frolic eye!
Innocence sits upon thy open brow,
 Like a pure spirit in its native sky.
If ever beauty stole the heart away,
 Enchantress, it would fly to meet thy smile;
Moments would seem by thee a summer day,
 And all around thee an Elysian isle.
Roses are nothing to the maiden blush
 Sent o'er thy cheek's soft ivory, and night
 Has naught so dazzling in its world of light,
As the dark rays that from thy lashes gush.
 Love lurks amid thy silken curls, and lies
 Like a keen archer in thy kindling eyes.

To Frederick Ryan

WILFRID SCAWEN BLUNT

Fabric of clay, poor, impotent child's face,
Ransomed from thought, its load of life laid down!
Earth of all earth, disrobed and passionless,
Dead mask of a man's brow, which once could frown,
Eyes which could smile, lips which could hold their own
Relentless against wrong in eloquent stress
Indignant at our English ill crop sown,
Curse of the World, its tares of bitterness!
—Kind Irish soul, free labourer in a field
Rich with rebellion's mint from age to age,
Young ever in revolt, and child–like still!
Are these thy wages then of sword and shield,
Naked to lie and never take thy fill
Of human pleasure, to the end thus sage?

RALPH ERSKINE

Much fam'd on earth, renown'd for piety;
Amidst bright seraphs now sings cheerfully.
Sacred thine anthems yield much pleasure here;
These songs of thine do truly charm the ear.
Each line thou wrot'st doth admiration raise;
Rouse up the soul to true seraphic praise.

Religiously thy life below was spent:
Amazing pleasures now thy soul content.
Long didst thou labour in the church below,
Pointing out Christ, the Lamb, who saves from woe,
Heav'n's blessedness on sinners to bestow.

Erskine the great! whose pen spread far abroad
Redeeming love, the sole device of God;
Substantial themes thy thoughts did much pursue;
Kept pure the truth, espous'd but by a few.
Integrity of heart, of soul serene;
No friend to vice, no cloak to the profane:
Employ'd thy talents to reclaim the vain.

CHARLES LAMB

Go, little poem, and present
Respectful terms of compliment,
A Gentle Lady bids thee speak;
Courteous is She, though Thou be weak.
Evoke from Heav'n, as thick as Manna,

Joy after joy, on Grace Joanna.
On Fornham's glebe and pasture land
A blessing pray. Long, long may stand,
Not touch'd by time, the Rectory blithe
No grudging churl dispute his tithe.
At Easter be the offerings due

With cheerful spirit paid. Each pew
In decent order fill'd. No noise
Loud intervene to drown the voice,
Learning or wisdom, of the Teacher.
Impressive be the Sacred Preacher,
And strict his notes on Holy Page.
May young and old from age to age
Salute and still point out the "Good Man's Parsonage."

JANE JOHNSTON SCHOOLCRAFT

A thing of glitter, gleam, and gold,
Loose thoughts, loose verse, unmeaning, old,
Big words that sound a thousand fold;
Unfinished scraps, conceit and cant,
Mad stanzas, and a world of rant.

Particular Acrostic

THOMAS JORDAN

Though crost in our affections, still the flames
Of Honour shall secure our noble Names;
Nor shall Our fate divorce our faith, Or cause
The least Mislike of love's Diviner lawes.
Crosses sometimes Are cures, Now let us prove,
That no strength Shall Abate the power of love:
Honour, wit, beauty, Riches, wise men call
Frail fortune's Badges, In true love lies all.
Therefore to him we Yield, our Vowes shall be
Paid — Read, and written in Eternity:
That All may know when men grant no Redress,
Much love can sweeten the unhappinesS.

Our Life Is Hid with Christ in God

GEORGE HERBERT

Colossians, III

MY words and thoughts do both express this notion,
That LIFE hath with the sun a double
The first IS straight, and our diurnal friend;
The other HID, and doth obliquely bend.
One life is wrapt IN flesh, and tends to earth:
The other winds towards HIM, whose happy birth
Taught me to live here so, THAT still one eye
Should aim and shoot at that which IS on high;
Quitting with daily labour all MY pleasure,
To gain at harvest an eternal TREASURE.

Acrostic: Georgiana Augusta Keats

JOHN KEATS

Give me your patience, sister, while I frame
Exact in capitals your golden name;
Or sue the fair Apollo and he will
Rouse from his heavy slumber and instill
Great love in me for thee and Poesy.
Imagine not that greatest mastery
And kingdom over all the Realms of verse,
Nears more to heaven in aught, than when we nurse
And surety give to love and Brotherhood.

Anthropophagi in Othello's mood;
Ulysses storm'd and his enchanted belt
Glow with the Muse, but they are never felt
Unbosom'd so and so eternal made,
Such tender incense in their laurel shade
To all the regent sisters of the Nine
As this poor offering to you, sister mine.

Kind sister! ay, this third name says you are;
Enchanted has it been the Lord knows where;
And may it taste to you like good old wine,
Take you to real happiness and give
Sons, daughters and a home like honied hive.

ROBERT BRIDGES

Pathetic strains and passionate they wove,
Urgent in ecstasies of heavenly sense;
Responsive rivalries that, while they strove,
Combined in full harmonious suspense,
Entrancing wild desire, then fell at last
Lulled in soft closes, and with gay contrast
Launched forth their fresh unwearied excellence.

Morn smiles in loveliness on many a flower,
In whose bright petals live the rainbows dyes,
Spreading its perfume round the dew-dropped bower,
Sweet tribute to the zephyr as it sighs.

How passing pure is evenings radiant star,
Ether its azure bed and tranquil home;
Bright, beautiful, it beams from heaven afar,
Dimpling with lustre the cerulean dome.
Oh! both are fair—but in thee both combine,
Now grace that cheek, and light those eyes of thine.

The Argument

BEN JONSON

The sickness hot, a master quit, for fear,
His house in town, and left one servant there.
Ease him corrupted, and gave means to know
A Cheater and his punk, who now brought low,
Leaving their narrow practice, were become
Coz'ners at large; and, only wanting some
House to set up, with him they here contract,
Each for a share, and all begin to act.
Much company they draw, and much abuse,
In casting figures, telling fortunes, news,
Selling of flies, flat bawdry, with the Stone;
Till it, and they, and all in fume are gone.

EPILOGUE: HIDDEN ACROSTICS BY SHAKESPEARE, MILTON, AND JOYCE

This volume focuses on poems that their authors doubtlessly intended to come across as acrostics. Three literary legends penned hidden acrostics: acrostics concealed within larger works.

William Shakespeare, dubbed the greatest dramatist of all time, employed hidden acrostics in two plays. In *A Midsummer Night's Dream*, the character Titania utters a speech where six lines spell out her name. The fourth line begins with "And," where the first two letters count toward her seven-letter name:

> Thou shalt remain here, whether thou wilt or no.
> I am a spirit of no common rate:
> The summer still doth tend upon my state;
> And I do love thee: therefore, go with me;
> I'll give thee fairies to attend on thee;
> And they shall fetch thee jewels from the deep,

In the wordplay magazine *Word Ways*, A. Ross Eckler provided a statistical analysis of whether the acrostic might have been inadvertent. He determined that because there is a "self-referential acrostic," Shakespeare "deliberately doctored this passage to spell out Titania's name."

In Shakespeare's *The Comedy of Errors*, the acrostic "Want My Baby" appears in a roundabout way:

> To bear the extremity of dire mishap!
> Now, trust me, were it not against our laws,
> Against my crown, my oath, my dignity,
> Which princes, would they, may not disannul,
> My soul should sue as advocate for thee.
> But, though thou art adjudged to the death,
> And passed sentence may not be recall'd
> But to our honour's great disparagement,
> Yet will I favour thee in what I can.

In *Word Ways*, James Kovalick explained:

> The first word reads backwards (upwards) from, and is just above, a central line that contains the second word . . . the third word reads forwards (downwards) from, and is just below, the central line. Aegeon, looking all over the world for his lost son (baby), wanders to this kingdom and is condemned to die. Before his death, he has the above interchange with the Duke, who sympathized with him, but cannot pardon him. In the very lines that the Duke is offering sympathy, Shakespeare is acrostically describing Aegeon's greatest desire—he wants his long-lost baby son!

Kovalick explored whether such an acrostic could have "occurred just by chance." He concluded, "Not if the word play fits into the context of what is being said."

John Milton's *Paradise Lost*, considered one of the greatest poems ever written in English, contains the following passage:

> Scipio, the highth of Rome. With tract oblique
> At first, as one who sought access but feared
> To interrupt, sidelong he works his way.
> As when a ship, by skilful steersmen wrought
> Nigh river's mouth or foreland, where the wind

"SATAN" is spelled out as part of a description of a serpent, which represents Satan. In *Milton Quarterly*, P. J. Klemp explained:

> If an acrostic appears in a long poem, it will be surrounded by hundreds of lines whose initial letters are in random order. In an epic, the context in which an acrostic appears must convince the reader that the configuration is not in fact a series of letters grouped only by coincidence. . . . Milton has fused form and content to produce an acrostic which acts in a way as a gloss upon the text. And this is no display of "false wit." The acrostic appears at a very dramatic moment in the narrative and is perfectly suited to its context.

Another *Milton Quarterly* article contended that five consecutive lines spelling out "STARS" also constitute a deliberate acrostic in *Paradise Lost*.

In *Ulysses*, arguably the best novel of the twentieth century, James Joyce included an explicitly labeled acrostic for "POLDY," a nickname of the protagonist, Leopold Bloom. In *James Joyce Quarterly*, Tristan Power posited that several of Joyce's poems feature acrostics. In poem XXVII in *Chamber Music*, the first letters of the final four lines spell out "NONE":

> Nor have I known a love whose praise
> > Our piping poets solemnize,
> Neither a love where may not be
> Ever so little falsity.

Power noted that this is fitting because "the lover knows no such love as he describes." Power speculated that Joyce "manipulated" an earlier version of the poem in order to incorporate this acrostic. The following poem in *Chamber Music* ends with the initial letters spelling out "SOIL." According to Power, since "the grave" is mentioned in the same passage, this "can hardly be a coincidence." In "Tutto è Sciolto" in *Pomes Penyeach*, the hidden acrostic "APART" "seems to be confirmed by the fact that it underscores the poem's theme—that of lost love," said Power.

Hidden acrostics do not succeed as stand-alone verse. They only have meaning in the context of other works. Leading writers have incorporated the acrostic form as an extra touch that some readers might notice.

SELECTED BIBLIOGRAPHY

This bibliography is not a complete record of all works and sources. Readers who are interested in the most significant literature about acrostic poetry should read the following.

Augarde, Tony. *The Oxford Guide to Word Games*. Oxford: Oxford University Press, 2003.

Blackwell, Robert. *Original Acrostics, on All the States and Presidents of the United States, and Various Other Subjects Religious, Political and Personal*. Cincinnati, 1868.

Chilton, W. P. *Columbia: A National Poem: Acrostic on the American Union: With Sonnets*. New York: The Authors' Publishing Company, 1880.

Chilton, W. P. *Mansions of the Skies: An Acrostic Poem on the Lord's Prayer*. New York: John Ross & Co., Publishers, 1875.

Fage, Mary. *Fames Roule: or, The Names of Our Dread Soveraigne Lord King Charles, His Royall Queen Mary, and His Most Hopefull Posterity: Together with, The Names of the Dukes, Marquesses, Earles, Viscounts, Bishops, Barons, Privie Counsellors, Knights of the Garter, and Judges. Of His Three Renowned Kingdomes, England, Scotland, and Ireland: Anagrammatiz'd and Expressed by Acrosticke Lines on Their Names*. London: Richard Oulton, 1637.

Grinfield, Charles Vaughan. *A Century of Acrostics on the Most Eminent Names in Literature, Science, and Art, Down to the Present Time: Chronologically Arranged*. London: Simpkin, Marshall & Co., 1855.

Hirsch, Edward. *The Essential Poet's Glossary*. Boston: Mariner Books, 2017.

Indictor, Nyr. "Alphabet Poems: A Brief History." *Word Ways* 28, no. 3 (1995): 131–5.

Krueger, Robert, ed. *The Poems of Sir John Davies*. London: Oxford University Press, 1975.

Lockerby, D. F. *Acrostical Pen Portraits of the Eighteen Presidents of the United States*. Philadelphia: J. L. Sibole, 1876.

O'Connor, J. E. *Acrostic Sonnets and Other Poems*. San Francisco: Progress Printing Co., 1916.

Partridge, Eric. *Comic Alphabets: Their Origin, Development, Nature.* London: Routledge & Kegan Paul, 1961.

Untermeyer, Louis. *The Pursuit of Poetry: A Guide to Its Understanding and Appreciation with an Explanation of Its Forms and a Dictionary of Poetic Terms.* New York: Simon and Schuster, 1969.

Wells, Carolyn, ed. *A Whimsey Anthology.* 1906. Reprint, New York: Dover Publications, 1963.